Maximize the Leader in You:

10 Strategies for Greater Success and Happiness

Teresa Shaffer

ISBN-13: 978-1492219262
ISBN-10: 1492219266

Table of Contents

Preface:
Why Read This Book?

Corporations today are steeped in high-change and high-stress that is happening at astounding speeds. Leaders must deliver better faster results, and at the same time, inspire and engage their people in this highly-competitive global marketplace.

People are the heartbeat of organizations and the primary competitive advantage. However, according to a highly respected study, an alarming number of employees are not showing up committed, engaged, or working to their full potential. Yesterday's leadership can no longer support the shifting world dynamics that are taking place today. We need a radically different approach.

The antidote to this challenge is to develop self-aware leaders who lead from a place of service, values and higher purpose, so people can flourish and reach their human potential for the greater good of organizations and humanity as a whole. The world is ready for a new leadership paradigm and more conscious leadership.

This book will begin to show you how to do this.

Maximize the Leader in You:
10 Strategies for Greater Success and Happiness

Introduction

Leadership has been a topic of fascination since the beginning of civilization, from the study of philosophers and Roman rulers to modern day heroes. I have been fascinated with leadership from the different models and theories to the lives of great leaders who are or were so uniquely gifted with different strengths and styles, yet all left a profound and positive difference in the world, such as Abraham Lincoln, Margaret Thatcher, Mother Teresa, Rosa Parks, and Martin Luther King. Then there are modern day thought leaders who have made a tremendously positive impact on leadership today, like Marshall Goldsmith, Linda Tarr-Whelan, and Daniel Goleman — all great teachers who have resonated with me personally.

Thinking back, I have been a leader from the young age of 14 when I played sports, encouraging a winning attitude on my basketball and track teams, leading emergencies as a nurse in life threatening situations, teaching 12-year-old children about teamwork, or building and leading teams in multi-million dollar sales divisions. This book is a practical guide based on many years observing and working for great leaders as well as my own leadership experiences, training, reading, and coaching. I've also witnessed the other side of the coin and have learned what not to do as a leader, which will not be discussed in here. I was passionate about leadership then, and I'm even more so now.

Which brings me to YOU!

You are a successful, intelligent executive or manager with high standards. You have extraordinary talents and strengths as a leader, as do your teams. Now, I want you, your teams, and organization to be even more successful!

Executives and managers have been given a great responsibility: the noble opportunity to be a leader. And you can always improve on the positive difference you're making, whether you're leading a team of 10 or 3000.

Today, there is an urgent call to lead with higher purpose, values and authenticity. These have been tough economic times. We can see there is a global crisis in leadership and this is a serious situation. Leading can be a tough job, overwhelming, even lonely at times. You are pulled in so many directions, expected to do more with less. This leaves many executives and managers finding themselves on autopilot, reacting to the events of the day, racing from one activity to another with little time to develop top talent, have meaningful conversations, connect, or reflect.

It is human nature to look for the magic bullet, a quick way to rise to the top, or an answer from the outside on how to instantly be better, especially when we are so busy. But the answer really starts on the inside with self-awareness and knowing who you are; with a commitment to excellence; and with the perseverance to follow through on your plan. I invite you to read, reflect, and do the written exercises in this book where you feel the need to do so. Leadership is a lifelong learning journey with many twists and turns, ups and downs. It is exciting, challenging, and rewarding. This is about taking an honest look at yourself. Really understanding what you do best and doing it better; enhancing capabilities; or changing just one behavior that could be holding you back from that next level of success or being more fulfilled in your career.

As you delve into this book, identify just one or two areas that will help you to be a more authentic, purpose driven and successful leader. Commit to a plan, set goals, and put small steps in place that you take every day for just 30 minutes for a minimum of 30 days—90 days preferably. And identify a support system of trustworthy, like-minded people who will hold you accountable to reaching your next goals. I believe writing down your goals and reviewing these goals every day, journaling, and enlisting a supportive team to help you stay committed and accountable will help you achieve your goals more quickly. Please do not forget to recognize milestones achieved and have some fun along the way.

I leave you with this last thought before you get started. You are dedicated, working many long hours, and maybe even neglecting personal time or hobbies that you enjoy. It is not the outside part that matters most or endures the test of time, but rather who you are becoming and who you are inside that matters most. So I ask you this: when you are 80 looking back at your life, what kind of leadership legacy will you leave behind? It is so important to remember your WHY — why you wanted to be a leader in the first place! Everyone wants to find meaning and purpose in their life? What is the difference you are trying to make in the world? What do you stand for? No one else has the same talent or gifts that you have to offer to the world. This is why you are here, to step courageously into your uniqueness and magnificence, and to help others do the same. You owe it to yourself, your team, your organization, and society itself to be your absolute best!

So let's begin.

Teresa

Teresa Shaffer, CEC, CPC
Shaffer Executive Coaching, LLC
www.ShafferExecutiveCoaching.com

Strategy #1: Know Thyself, Practice Your Values

Aspiring to become your best as a leader starts with the work you do on the inside and to understanding who you are and what you believe. This helps you lead yourself, others, and organizations with greater authenticity. Your values must be clearly communicated to your team because this is what you stand for and will help your team understand you better and work together with greater clarity, meaning and purpose.

Values are deep beliefs — collectively a philosophy that is personally meaningful to you. Values can be ideals that improve your life, the lives of your employees or team members, and the lives of your customers and humanity as a whole. Some of your values can of course change over time, especially as you begin to understand yourself better. These can include altruism and compassion, integrity and contribution, competence and achievement, freedom and honesty, and so on.

Values provide a framework. They are like a compass that guides your decisions and behaviors and help keep you from taking the wrong path, especially when you are under pressure. Your most significant contribution is not only short term results and the bottom line but to the long term sustainability of the organization and the development of people, knowing they are the heartbeat of an organization. Values also define 'how' you do something, not 'what' you do. When you understand your value system and live congruently with your values, then you will feel more energized and inspired. If there have been times when you end up feeling frustrated, drained, maybe even anxious and you're just not sure why, it could be because you're not living in harmony with your values.

One example of a core value is Connectedness. A person with this value wouldn't choose to be around negative and self-serving people. When this value of Connectedness is not honored, the individual lives with incongruence, and most likely will feel it in a variety of ways, such as stress, loss of motivation, less happiness, or the feeling that it's time to move on.

Two of my values are Contribution and Growth. It is so important for me to contribute to the betterment of people, organizations and society by optimizing and sharing my unique talents and strengths. I continuously strive to learn, grow, and give my absolute best so I contribute to bring unmatched value to those I serve. I have a tremendous respect for diversity and inclusion, which need to be realized and given the opportunity to thrive. Honoring diversity and inclusion is about leveraging the collective talents, perspectives, and unique leadership styles to achieve organizational excellence and make workplaces stronger. It will be a social and business imperative to leverage talent across gender, culture, thinking and generations because it is this diversity that propels us forward in today's rapidly changing global marketplace. This is about shared responsibility in which everyone's contributions are meaningful and valuable in lifting organizations to a higher plane. This requires conscious thought and action to create this type of workplace. I am unrelentingly committed to supporting the growth and unique talents of others so they can unleash their brilliance and step into their full potential. Living my values of Contribution and Growth brings purpose, meaning, and happiness to my life.

Some individuals have never identified their top values, but it is never too late. In our day to day lives, we are so busy that we move through each day in this unconscious awareness, and our behaviors sometimes reflect this unconsciousness. Let's face it: it's difficult to keep up with the daily demands of our life, let alone to find time for self-discovery and reflection. But it's important to bring your values into conscious awareness because understanding what you believe in, what is driving you today, and why you do what you do will help you live a more fulfilled and inspired life, both personally and professionally.

Personal values are the foundation of a more fulfilling, satisfying, and successful life.

Values affect the decisions you make and influence the goals you want to achieve. The first step in leading with our values is defining what those values are. Once we start paying attention and defining them, we begin thinking of our values in new terms and with new priorities. Again, it's important to identify the values that are true to you, not what you think your values should be by someone else's standards.

I recommend thinking of this as an exciting opportunity rather than a task or chore, because it doesn't take a lot of time or effort all at once, and as your values are better defined, it becomes easier to define goals, push through challenges, and make business decisions from them. All this makes work more gratifying on a daily basis, and makes long-term success more satisfying as well.

As you hone in on values with real meaning to you, on those that hold the *most* importance, you can start to reflect on them before making business decisions. This can include who you hire, how you build your teams, and how you attract customers who respond to these values. This promotes better experiences for you and others, and fuels your passion to lead within your business.

Remember, the values you claim must be true to you and match your actions. You must walk the talk or you'll lose credibility as a leader. Knowing your values and building your life around these values help create a life that is more fulfilling and satisfying.

Key Points:

- Values are deep beliefs that are personally meaningful and unique to you.
- Values provide a framework. They are like the compass that guides your choices and behaviors and help you from taking the wrong path especially when you are under pressure.
- Values define 'how' you do something not 'what' you do.
- It is important to bring your values into conscious awareness because understanding who you are, what you believe, and why you do what you do will help you live a more fulfilling, successful, and happier life, both personally and professionally.

Written Exercises:

1. Take out a piece of paper or a journal. As you first venture into defining your core values, write down all those that come to mind if they're important to you. Do this *before* looking at any lists of values. If you rely on a list, you may forget something most meaningful to you; at the same time, using a list after your initial effort can add some key terms for you.

_____

_____

_____

_____

_____

2. Another way of reflecting on your most cherished values is to think of a personal and/or leadership experience that meant a great deal to you.

    a. Think about those experiences and see if they represented one or more values you listed in question 1. Write specific evidence on how your actions matched your values.

_____

_____

_____

_____

_____

b. What were the challenges if your actions didn't match your values? How did you feel when they did or didn't match?

_____

_____

_____

_____

_____

_____

_____

c. Think about business/team decisions that you recently made. What values did you use? Do your values depend on the situation you are facing? Do your personal values align with company values? Why or why not? If not, what can you do to resolve this conflict?

_____

_____

_____

_____

_____

_____

_____

3. Once you have a list of your top 10 values, narrow the list to your top 5 core values in rank order from most important to least important. How do your values shape your beliefs? Describe how these values are important to you and how they impact your life and career choices.

_____

_____

_____

_____

_____

_____

Possible Values:

- ☐ Accountability
- ☐ Achievement
- ☐ Adventure
- ☐ Ambition
- ☐ Autonomy
- ☐ Caring
- ☐ Challenge
- ☐ Communication
- ☐ Compassion
- ☐ Connectedness
- ☐ Courage
- ☐ Creativeness
- ☐ Curiosity
- ☐ Discovery
- ☐ Diversity
- ☐ Empathy
- ☐ Excellence
- ☐ Fairness/Justice
- ☐ Freedom
- ☐ Fun

- ☐ Giving back/ Generosity
- ☐ Gratitude
- ☐ Growth/Learning
- ☐ Happiness
- ☐ Humility
- ☐ Inclusion
- ☐ Innovation
- ☐ Integrity/Honesty
- ☐ Love
- ☐ Open mindedness
- ☐ Optimal wellbeing
- ☐ Optimism
- ☐ Purpose-driven
- ☐ Risk taking
- ☐ Service to Others
- ☐ Teamwork
- ☐ Transparency
- ☐ Trustworthy
- ☐ Understanding

- ☐ Uniqueness
- ☐ Wholeness
- ☐ _____
- ☐ _____
- ☐ _____
- ☐ _____
- ☐ _____
- ☐ _____
- ☐ _____

Chapter Reflections and Notes

_____

_____

_____

_____

_____

_____

_____

_____

_____

_____

_____

_____

Strategy #2:
Lead from Strengths

We all know that if we find something we love to do, we "never have to work a day in our lives." People gladly do the things they enjoy, and focusing on strengths is a big part of this. If we're good at something, we can succeed with it; if we can succeed with it, we usually feel great about it.

So it's surprising that many leaders don't focus on connecting their people with the things they're good at. Instead, they call attention to faults and insist that people spend precious work hours improving on things they'll never be great at. They then lose confidence, and the process creates a workforce full of mediocrity — "jacks of all trades and masters of none."

Why build a workforce of average people when you could build a workforce of masters?

I have seen the error of focusing on weaknesses first hand when taking over teams whose previous leaders did exactly that. They had people on improvement plans, leaving them fearful of losing their jobs. Of course there are many causes of mediocre or poor performance, but I've found that many times it's easier to turn this around by focusing on strengths.

It's also a whole lot more fun as a leader, because frankly, it's incredibly frustrating to lead people by focusing on their weaknesses. It's like getting angry at the lawn mower for being so difficult to use in trimming the shrubs. It's not made for that. Put it to work on the lawn.

The research really backs all of this up. We learn in books like *Now, Find Your Strengths* and *Strengths Finder 2.0* that we gain far more excellence and production in the workplace by building on people's strengths than we can by trying to correct their weaknesses. In the book *Strengths Based Leadership*, Tom Rath points out that individuals don't necessarily need to be well rounded. That's the job of teams. Allowing individuals to build on strengths generates a lot more confidence, happiness, and goodwill ... and far fewer days away from work.

Of course as a leader, this begins with YOU. We shouldn't believe that all leaders need the same style or skills, so there's no need to try mimicking someone else. The strongest leaders discover who they are, what they love, and what they're good at, and they apply all this to the benefit of those they lead and the company they work for. They then help their people do the same, causing a chain reaction of greatness.

Certainly this doesn't mean we ignore personal development. Someone's strengths today will not, by themselves, give them everything needed to move from individual contributor to management to executive positions. But even then, it makes sense to leverage your strengths when developing new skills, as well as seeing where your weaknesses are (one reason self-reflection is so important!) and surrounding yourself with those who can fill in the gaps. Doing this also gives you the opportunity to learn from those people, which betters help you in turning your weaknesses into assets, even if you will never be the expert in that area.

But besides developing our own weaknesses, that idea of filling in the gaps — putting the right people together — is key to managing weak areas. You're essentially putting the puzzle together — putting together teams where individual strengths complement individual weaknesses. After all, if you force everyone to be a circle (everyone's good at the same things), the puzzle you build will have gaps in the picture and will never stay connected. Sometimes leaders surround themselves with others who have strengths, thinking, and behavior like themselves. This stifles the growth of the leader, employees, and organization. Allowing strengths to arise and to lock arms lets you build a more complete puzzle image and promotes happy teams and results that will last.

One of my favorite summaries of this point comes from Tom Rath and Barry Conchie in *Strengths Based Leadership*:

1) The most effective leaders are always investing in strengths.

2) The most effective leaders surround themselves with the right people and then maximize their team.

3) The most effective leaders understand their followers' needs.

By leveraging strengths, you will also have a great opportunity to elevate engagement, excitement, accountability, and productivity because you are getting everyone engaged, rather than leaving people out. A leader who embraces diverse talents and strengths puts people where they will shine. You are taking what you do best and doing it better, then helping others do the same so everyone can flourish.

Key Points:

- Consider what you love doing, and what you do well.
- Spend more time building on those strengths and aim to use strengths every day.
- Empower your team members to do the same.
- Build teams so that one person's strengths complement another person's weaknesses.
- By leveraging strengths, you will have a great opportunity to elevate engagement, excitement, accountability, and productivity because you are getting everyone engaged rather than leaving people out.
- Taking what you do best and do it better, then help others do the same so everyone can flourish.

Written Exercises:

1. What are your top 5 strengths as a leader? (To help leaders identify their leadership strengths, Clifton and his Gallup researchers developed The StrengthsFinder program. Purchase Clifton StrengthsFinder access codes at: www.strengthstest.com.)

_____

_____

_____

_____

_____

_____

2. What are each of your team members' top 5 strengths?

_____

_____

_____

_____

_____

_____

_____

_____

_____

_____

3. How can you link individual and team strengths to organizational goals and projects to achieve outstanding results for the employee and organization?

_____

_____

_____

_____

_____

4. Assess your effectiveness from 1-10 — with 10 being very effective, 5 being effective, and 1 being ineffective — in maximizing your strengths and employee strengths. Put an "Action Plan" in place to improve your effectiveness in leading based on strengths.

_____

_____

_____

_____

_____

_____

_____

_____

_____

Chapter Reflections and Notes

_____

_____

_____

_____

_____

_____

_____

_____

_____

_____

_____

_____

_____

Strategy #3:
Build Strong Teams

Imagine trying to win a football game with a team full of quarterbacks and you instantly understand why success in any field means pulling together a group whose members complement one another. A good quarterback calls plays, reads the defense, passes, and may run from time to time. But his expertise isn't in running or catching the ball, and he would get crushed by opposing linemen. Football teams need quarterbacks, but they also need people who are good at all of the other positions.

I talk about leading from your own strengths and allowing others to develop their own strengths as well. While this leaves gaps in one's individual armor — one person may not have all the skills to run a successful company — it allows teams to come together and fill in those gaps. With each person bringing his or her own "A" game, the team works from a place of strength rather than a place of mediocrity.

But there's more to building strong teams than fitting together strengths. For one thing, as Jon Katzenbach and Douglas Smith of *The Wisdom of Teams* point out, setting ambitious performance standards helps to build strong teams because members have a common purpose and recognize that they can better meet these standards as a team than they can as individuals. This creates more commitment to the team concept than simply telling people they are a team and trying to convince them that they have a common goal.

Even then, of course, you can put all the right skills together and still have a team that fails because there are other elements to humans working together. We like and dislike people for personality reasons; or we may or may not communicate well with them.

We can't necessarily fix likes and dislikes, but we can still create a high performance team.

As you start to build an atmosphere of trust, communication, accountability, and recognition for success, people who didn't click at first could become friendly and start to connect and become inspired. I have found from my own experience and from other top leaders that after you have hired well, building and leading high performing teams requires a leader to do the following:

Integrity. In the book, *Integrity* by Stephen Carter, he writes, "a person of integrity lurks inside each of us: a person we feel we can trust to do right thing, to play by the rules, to keep commitments, perhaps the first among the virtues that make for good character." Stephen Covey in *The Speed of Trust* states, "A person has integrity when there is no gap between intent and behavior....when he or she is whole, seamless, the same inside and out. This is congruency which will ultimately create credibility and trust."

Trust. The definition of trust in the Webster's new World College Dictionary is a "firm belief or confidence in the honesty, integrity, reliability, etc. of another person or thing; faith; reliance." First, you must have self-trust, a deep trust in who you are and the talent you bring to the world. Self-trust also means keeping promises to yourself before you can build trusting relationships in your organization. Trust is hard to build, easy to destroy. Building trust is a key competency for leaders and the foundation of a high performing team.

Here are some actions that build trust: develop your team; give credit and don't badmouth employees behind their backs because you don't have the courage to give tough feedback directly; understand and listen before you speak; when you make a mistake, learn to come from a place of humility instead of ego and pride; apologize and correct what you did wrong to the best of your ability. As a leader, communicate clearly, declare your intent, be honest, and walk-the-talk. When trust is the foundation of relationships, teams can experience unparalleled success, prosperity, and well-being.

Vision inspires employees to see they are contributing to something bigger than themselves. It shows people how they fit into this big picture, and why they should care. Leaders show "here's where we are going and why." This is the difference that our vision will make in the world.

Strategy. For this book, I will assume you have the right people in place. You have looked at the big picture, the 30,000 foot view. The strategies, SWOT, goals, and objectives are clearly defined to drive results. Effective and efficient processes and metrics are in place. The big picture has been broken down into smaller, pragmatic steps. So now it is time for you and your team to 'Get the Job Done.'

Follow through is critical. This is where the rubber meets the road and often where the ball is dropped. A leader's days are overwhelming and a constant race against the clock. It is easy to lose focus. One pitfall I have seen over and over is inattention to the plan. Many excellent strategic plans collect dust: out of sight, out of mind. If this is the case, you can bet your team is doing the same. Teams respect what you inspect.

Peter Drucker reminds us that management is doing things right; leadership is doing the right things. Following through on business a plan is one of those right things and will be one of the things I can assure you will separate average from top performance. Follow through is one of the critical keys to success and must become a habit, even if tedious, requiring discipline and accountability.

High performance leaders do the following with consistency when executing plans:

- Keep plans front and center and demand that their team do the same.
- Stay focused on their Highest Value Priorities that drive profitability.
- Don't disappear when the going gets tough, then come back when the challenges are resolved. Help clear obstacles, secure resources, and be available to listen and understand when momentum slows or tough problems arise. Be ready to roll up your sleeves, be a sounding board, or call your team together for collective brainstorming to solve a problem.
- Colin Powell's Leadership Lesson #5: "Never neglect details. When everyone's mind is dulled or distracted the leader must be doubly vigilant." Leaders must have obsessive processes in place to identify and close gaps, track milestones, measure objectives, and keep performance indicators top of mind while expecting the same from others.
- Communicate on a regular basis, week-to-week and month-to-month. Look for trends so you can respond appropriately and quickly to obstacles. Find ways to continuously improve.
- Tie incentives and rewards into strategic goals.

Accountability is another trust builder, and this applies not only to your team but to you as the leader as well. Accountability has two requirements: first, to not shirk one's own responsibilities; and second, to support the shared goals of the team by extending oneself and supporting other team members in their efforts. A leader needs to ensure that there are clear expectations, roles, and responsibilities and that everyone is on board.

Know and develop your people. The relationship you have with your direct reports is critically important. Take the time to get to know your people: their talents, strengths, motivators, career aspirations, communication styles, and other insights. A leader's number one responsibility is to develop talent and leaders in the organization. Jack Welch said, "My main job was developing talent. I was a gardener providing water and other nourishment to our top 750 people." The more you can develop your people and their competence, connecting their strengths/talents to an organization's short- and long-term goals, the more likely you will engage and deepen commitment of employees. Everyone wins in this situation: you, the individual, and the organization all grow and become stronger, moving to bigger opportunities and sustainability.

Show people you care. There are many ways to do this, and this is not a sign of a soft but rather a courageous leader. Further reading on this in Strategy #6, "Lead with the Heart." There are enough studies to show that employees care about the relationship they have with their boss and want to know they matter and contribute. It really is about the golden rule: treat others as you expect to be treated.

Commitment to excellence. Do your best and expect the best in return from your team. Leaders who build a strong foundation of trust and keep the bar at excellence for oneself and every single team member, this is what I see happen:

1.) You instill confidence in others, giving them a heightened sense of confidence to raise their own bar and encourage their peers to keep their bar high.

2.) You lead to a high performance team because you are raising others self-confidence and self-esteem. You are showing that you believe in your people; hence, you are creating a Pygmalion effect. You are creating a space for them to step into their full talent.

3) Then you will see an increase in performance of the entire team, especially from middle performers. The result: a win-win for everyone with a more confident, successful, and happy team!

A couple other points, keep in mind that as a leader you don't need all the answers or to prove you are always right. This can hold a team back from growth and development. However, you do need to have an unwavering commitment to unlock the potential and talents of your employees so they can be and do their best. Commitment to excellence requires discipline, hard work, and perseverance. Expect that mistakes will be made. Let your people know mistakes are OK. Celebrate mistakes when you see individuals grow and flourish because they took a courageous, calculated risk. Don't hold it against them for it. Instead, encourage your teams to continuously improve, stretch, and grow from their mistakes so they can move forward to play a bigger game.

Adjust your leadership style. Be flexible. It's important to adapt your leadership approach to different cultures, generations, situations, strengths, and skill sets.

Recognizing and having an awareness to adjust your leadership style requires emotional intelligence and empathy, which we will talk about in another part of this book. Keep in mind that as an employee's needs and situation change, your leadership style must change as well. Sometimes, I need to coach leaders to adjust their leadership style to the individual because it's far more effective t o be flexible, especially as diverse as the workforce is today.

Reward/Recognition is a basic human need, and it lets us know that others have seen our work and that our contribution matters. We are fueled by acknowledgement and recognition, and these inspire people to reach and surpass their own goals. However, recognition is often overlooked and employees feel unappreciated. As a leader, find out how your employees like to be recognized. Some prefer private recognition and others like public recognition. Either way, make it unique to the person and her/his contribution.

To make sure you get this done, create criteria, goals, and action plans for employee recognition. This will help you to more consistently recognize the competencies, behaviors, strengths, and accomplishments that you want to foster and reinforce in your organization.

Key Points:

- Build a team with complementary strengths and leverage these strengths.
- Stephen Covey in *The Speed of Trust* states, "A person has integrity when there is no gap between intent and behavior....when he or she is whole, seamless, the same inside and out. This is congruency which will ultimately create credibility and trust."
- Always build trust in developing a team. Building trust begins with self-trust and continues with factors like communication and showing people you care.
- Commit to excellence. High expectations lead to a high performance team because you are raising others self-confidence and self-esteem. You are showing you believe in your people. The result: a win-win for everyone leading to a confident, successful, and happy team.
- Inspire a vision and set clear strategies and outcomes. Accountability applies to every team member, including the leader. Define clear expectations, roles, and responsibilities. Employees respect what you measure and inspect.
- Follow through of business plans (execution) is a critical key to success.
- Know your people and adjust your leadership style for maximum impact.
- Reward and recognize competencies, behaviors and accomplishments that you want to reinforce in the organization with consistency, but also make it unique to the individual.

Written Exercises:

1. Keep a file on each direct report. Understand and really know the following on each member.

a. Talents, strengths, and development areas.

_____

_____

_____

_____

_____

b. Communication, learning, and thinking styles.

_____

_____

_____

_____

_____

c. What motivates the employees? How do they like to be recognized?

_____

_____

_____

_____

_____

d. What are their career goals?

_____

_____

_____

_____

_____

_____

_____

_____

2. A title doesn't necessarily give you the right to lead. You have to earn it. Seek advice on how you can be a better leader. There are many ways to do this: assessments, one-on-one meetings, asking great questions, keeping an open door policy. Put an action plan in place on one behavior you can change from employee feedback.

_____

_____

_____

_____

_____

_____

_____

_____

_____

_____

3. Rate your leadership effectiveness on a scale of 1-10 — with 10 being very effective, 5 being effective, and 1 being ineffective — on your company's leadership competencies. Put an action plan in place to improve one competency and track your progress.

_____

_____

_____

_____

_____

_____

_____

4. Take a course to help you lead teams more effectively. Examples include Situational Leadership or Emotional Intelligence workshops. Then apply what you learn and practice, practice, practice.

_____

_____

_____

_____

_____

_____

_____

Chapter Reflections and Notes

_____

_____

_____

_____

_____

_____

_____

_____

_____

_____

_____

_____

_____

_____

_____

_____

_____

_____

_____

_____

_____

_____

Strategy #4:
Share the Vision

While building strong teams does involve bringing the right kinds of talents or skills together, this doesn't always build a team that will last. Think about this: if you asked a bunch of people to gather in a public park for no reason, no one would show up. But if you offered a fireworks show in the park, you'd have crowds. In a similar way, leaders need to provide their teams with a *reason* for tackling their work. They need to set a vision for people to rally around, getting them ready and willing to contribute their skills to fulfilling that vision.

Now of course you could just get people showing up by offering money. And to a point, you can get people to commit themselves more deeply by offering more money. But research has shown time and again that money alone only goes so far in motivating people. Too often, businesses seem to think that giving out paychecks means they can expect anything they want from employees. But more than just needing money for food and shelter, people need to feel that they're contributing to something bigger than them-selves, and this is why the quality leader uses vision.

There is an intrinsic desire for people to feel that they are contributing to something bigger than themselves. This is the stage that leaders need to set.

Importantly, the leader who has already established personal values and is aligned with the company values that should be promoted in the workplace has a foundation to work from when setting the vision. **Corporate Values** are the ideals that drive decision making and dictate behavior and how people interact with each other. Values keep leaders and their teams grounded especially when pressure mounts. **Purpose** is why you exist and the positive difference you're trying to make in the world.

Vision is future oriented and describes what the organization will leave the world by living their purpose. Vision paints for the group where the organization is going, how employees fit into the big picture, and what it can look like when that execution happens. This gives focus and direction. Once the purpose and vision is there and team members are motivated to achieve that vision, then a leader can help a team to form a mission, strategies, goals, and a plan that make it all happen. The **Mission** answers the question, "How will we achieve this?"

Though not an example from business, one of the great examples of painting a vision comes from perhaps the most moving American speeches of the 20th century, Dr. King's "I Have a Dream." In his speech, he described his dream with incredible detail, suggesting how "former slaves and the sons of former slave owners" would be able "to sit down together at the table of brotherhood." King's speech inspired action in others then and to this day. His example of giving others something specific to strive for — something bigger than themselves — is a heart-felt example for a leader of any group to follow.

Key Points:

- **Corporate Values** are the ideals that drive decision making and dictate behavior and how people interact with each other.
- **Purpose** is why you exist and the positive difference you're trying to make in the world.
- **Vision** is future oriented and describes what the organization will leave the world by living their purpose. The leader needs to set the stage and paint the picture that people are contributing to something bigger than themselves. This gives focus and direction.
- Once the vision is articulated and team members are motivated to achieve that vision, *then* a leader can help a team to form a **mission**, specific strategies, goals, and a plan of action to bring the vision to life.

- The **Mission** answers the question, "How will we achieve this?"

Written Exercises:

1. What is your organization's purpose? What is the vision for the future? What is your message to inspire your team to rally behind this vision? How will your employees act, think, feel when they contribute to this vision?

---

2. What is your organization's mission statement? What top 3 strategies and priorities must you do in order to succeed this year and contribute to the company vision and mission? What milestones do you need to measure, recognize and reward?

---

3. What are the corporate values? What non-negotiable values and principles define how you and your team work to accomplish these goals around this vision?

Chapter Reflections and Notes

_____

_____

_____

_____

_____

_____

_____

_____

_____

_____

_____

_____

_____

_____

_____

_____

_____

_____

Strategy #5:
Develop Emotional
Intelligence

Like it or not, no one simply packs up their computer bag and heads to work leaving emotions at home. Emotions are part of being a human being, but they can be considered to be taboo at work. Within the organizational culture, there is also a definite culture of emotion that comes with rules. Rules that people learn very quickly. Yet not everyone has the natural Emotional Intelligence, or EQ, to make the most of human and organizational emotion.

Emotional Intelligence isn't about sweet sentiments written in a Hallmark card. Emotional Intelligence is based on years of research by scientists. It is about being aware of and managing our emotions and working more effectively with others to improve relationships and performance. In our current economic climate, with merged and downsized workforces, business environments are filled with high stress and high change. We need Emotionally Intelligent leaders more than ever.

Daniel Goleman is the thought leader on this topic. In his article, "What Makes a Leader?" Goleman discusses how we've all probably worked with the very intelligent executive who has the right credentials and technical skills, yet who performs at an average level and sometimes fails. Then there is the executive with average intelligence who rises to be a great leader. So we ask the question: *what is the difference between these two leaders?*

There is plenty of research to show that Emotional Intelligence — more so than IQ — can make a significant impact in organizations, from leaders who drive greater profits to salespeople who drive more sales, develop better customer relationships, and who perform better overall. So what can give organizations the competitive advantage in this highly competitive global market?

In his book, *Working with Emotional Intelligence*, Goleman reports that 80-90% of the competencies that differentiate top performers are in the domain of Emotional Intelligence. The author suggests five competencies that we can develop: Self Awareness, Self-Regulation, Motivation, Empathy, and Social skills.

What does the leader look like with high EQ? These leaders are aware of their emotions, values, and motivators. They're confident in their strengths and know how to manage their weaknesses. These leaders are ambitious, but are more inspired by intrinsic motivators — making a positive difference, developing talent, and building a strong loyalty base with the organization and customers.

These leaders also self regulate, meaning they can control their emotions, thinking clearly and calmly before they act, especially under pressure. They can look beyond their own self interest and see the bigger picture. They can deal with change and uncertainty effectively while helping others to do the same. They are optimistic and empathetic, aim to understand other people, and appreciate individuality so they are comfortable with diversity. They can influence, adjust their leadership style, and inspire and encourage employees to achieve a shared vision. And they have strong social skills.

The interesting point is that business desperately wants everything to be logical, analytical, and focused on a cerebral approach, cut off from emotions because they are too "soft." I certainly respect my logical mind, and I enjoy solving problems with it. When I was in charge of the unit as a nurse, I remember being so eager to learn and make rounds with the chief physician, teaching resident physicians about the latest research or how to gather different data points to diagnosis a rare disease or save a life in an emergency.

However, there is more to success than the linear mind. When you can step in another's shoes, empathizing and understanding people's thoughts and feelings, you will ignite a human spark of connection. One of my best supervisors was in my career as a nurse. In retrospect, I can see why she rose to executive leadership status with a loyal following and garnered such positions as Chief Officer Nurse and VP in leading US Health Care Systems. She was very intelligent, logical, and visionary. Yet, she also had a high EQ, a big heart, empathy, and a gift for developing talent in others. She was responsive to the feelings and needs of those around her in the hospital.

As marketing expert Seth Godin points out, when we make people commodities and remove the human element from business, we're in a race to the bottom, looking to compete only on price. And Warren Bennis, renowned leadership pioneer, author and researcher makes this point: "In the fields I have studied, emotional intelligence is much more powerful than IQ in determining who emerges as a leader." As we master EQ, we can connect the world of logic and emotion, bringing the human element into business for greater satisfaction, stronger relation-ships, and better bottom line results.

EQ joins logic and emotion for more satisfying professional and personal effectiveness and results.

As leaders, then, we need to be comfortable or start *getting* comfortable with our own emotions by starting to further develop the 5 key EQ skills. With commitment, training, practice, and feedback, EQ can be learned and improved. By doing this, we set the example for others on the team. We create an environment where emotional intelligence can improve leadership as well as personal and professional effectiveness.

Key Points:

- In his book, *Working with Emotional Intelligence*, Goleman reports that 80-90% of the competencies that differentiate top performers are in the domain of emotional intelligence.
- Goleman suggests five competencies that we can develop: Self Awareness, Self-Regulation, Motivation, Empathy, and Social Skills.
- With commitment, training, practice, and feedback, EQ can be learned and improved. This sets the example and promotes greater effectiveness.

Written Exercises:

1. For 30 days, keep a journal and write about happy moments, stressful events, and tough conversations. The key is to bring awareness to how you feel in different situations so you can manage your emotions more effectively. Do not judge your emotions as good or bad. Just notice them because they are telling you something important. It is best to capture the feeling in the moment.

   a. What emotions were you feeling? Where are you feeling it in your body? (Heart racing, knot in your stomach, tension headache?) What triggered these emotions and reactions to others and why? How did your mood affect others?

---

b. After 1 month, identify your unique patterns and triggers that cause certain feelings and reactions? How can you better manage these triggers especially when you are stressed or fatigued?

_____

_____

_____

_____

_____

2. Take a baseline EQ assessment. Choose one skill and one strategy, then track and practice them for three months.

_____

_____

_____

_____

_____

3. How can you create a more emotionally intelligent team or organizational culture? How can your boss or organization support development in EQ?

_____

_____

_____

_____

_____

Chapter Reflections and Notes

_____

_____

_____

_____

_____

_____

_____

_____

_____

_____

_____

_____

_____

_____

_____

_____

_____

_____

Strategy #6:
Lead with the Heart

I talked about the importance of Emotional Intelligence, or EQ. This covers the whole range of people's emotions (yours as a leader included) and social relationships within the workplace. Among the important elements of this, we need to lead with the heart ... to remember that, like us, every team member has a personal and very human life. They have hopes and fears, goals and frustrations, the need to feel safe (e.g., trusting those around them), the need to contribute to something meaningful, and the need to be recognized for their contributions.

Leaders set a vision, inspire and build confidence, and bring out the absolute *best* in people to achieve this vision. This requires one to lead with both the head and the heart. Leading with the heart isn't soft stuff, but takes real courage and strength on the part of the leader. When executives lead not only with the head (thinking, strategy, and technical skills) but from the heart as well (feelings, trust, optimism, and empathy), employees will connect with the leader's humanness while feeling empowered to be their best and achieve exceptional results. Bringing your heart to work as a leader means showing people you care about them, their goals, and their success, and it gets people lined up to make great things happen.

In short, people need to be loved. Not a word we usually use in business, but after food and safety, love really encompasses all the words we typically use for human needs, like belonging, trust, support, and being cared for as individuals. Defined like this, the word love is really something we *should* be able to use as leaders! When people feel valuable as individuals and as team members, they're more likely to invest themselves in their work and in the company. We certainly need this in today's organizations.

As a leader, you can show you care by doing something as simple as sending a genuine handwritten note, recognizing an accomplishment, or celebrating a win with a team celebration dinner. In some cases, I offered myself for more serious situations such as sitting at the bedside of a colleague while receiving chemotherapy or seeking company approval to write a memorial with a scholarship fund for a little boy who lost his mother — one of my direct reports — to cancer.

I've also been fortunate to observe senior leaders who lead with their heart. They go out of their way to mentor, sponsor, share their wisdom, sponsor, mentor and create opportunities for others. They are exceptional leaders. I hope you too have sponsors, mentors, and coaches with heart. If not, it is never too late to develop these kinds of relationships. I believe it is time that we lead with a radically different approach, showing those who we work with that we genuinely care about their success; letting them know their talent and work is valued and that they matter as human beings.

After food and safety, love really encompasses all the words we typically use for human needs.

In their report "Engage Employees and Boost Performance,"[1] the Hay Group shows how touching on the motivations of employees and making them feel important increases not only their performance, but also the "discretionary effort" they're willing to put into their work — by up to 120%. The report also tells us: "*Fortune* magazine's 'America's Most Admired Companies' increased stock appreciation 50 percent over their peers because they instituted pro-employee measures."

Mark Crowley, who wrote *Lead from the Heart*, gives an example of how his efforts to guide team members from the heart (supporting their career goals, recognizing achievements, and so on) allowed him to also challenge them toward goals

---

[1] http://www.haygroup.com/downloads/us/engaged_performance_120401.pdf

substantially beyond those set by the company – and to *reach* those goals because they were motivated to do what others would not.

Another great leader who used these strategies was Andy Pearson, founding chairman and former CEO of Tricon Global Restaurants Inc. (which includes KFC, Pizza Hut, and Taco Bell). Andy developed a reputation over several decades as a ruthless, hard-nosed, numbers-obsessed success in corporate America.

However, he eventually came to realize that the need for recognition and approval is a fundamental human drive and is key to inspirational motivation. Pearson now leads by knowing the importance of the human heart in driving a company's success — one person at a time — and how this kind of success can't be imposed from the top, but must be ignited and nurtured through attention, awareness, recognition, and reward.

Key Points:

- Leading with the heart takes real courage and strength on the part of the leader. When executives lead not only with the head (thinking, strategy, and technical skills) but from the heart as well (feelings, trust, optimism, and empathy), employees will connect with the leader's humanness while feeling empowered to achieve exceptional results.
- Studies show that people will put themselves into the business more when their emotional needs are met. Caring for them helps you lead them into getting more done.
- Leading with heart can be ignited and nurtured through attention, awareness, recognition, and reward.
- Employees want to know they matter and that their work is valued.

Written Exercises:

1. How often do you personalize recognition and say "thank you" for a job well done? How do you show employees they are valued and that their contribution matters? What is one behavior you **need to stop** that undermines you as leader and gives others the perception that you don't really care? What is one behavior that you **can start** this week if you need to improve in this area?

_____

_____

_____

_____

_____

2. Write your employees' names on one side of a sheet of paper. On the other side, write down what motivates them. If you are not sure, when will you have a conversation to find out? Know what motivates every person on your team and then act on it and incorporate this into your coaching.

_____

_____

_____

_____

_____

_____

3. Send personal handwritten notes for birthdays; recognizing a milestone achieved; or thanking your employee's spouse, especially when long hours have taken their loved one away from family. Write ideas here.

_____

_____

_____

_____

_____

4. Think back to a time when a boss inspired you in a way that really touched your heart. What did she/he do? What words were used? How did it make you feel? How do you do the same for your employee?

_____

_____

_____

_____

_____

_____

_____

_____

_____

_____

Chapter Reflections and Notes

Strategy #7:
Build Authentic Relationships

The ability to be an effective and authentic leader is built on the relationships we develop over time, including the business and personal contacts we acquire in our organizations and com-munities. Cultivating these relationships is critical to our ability to influence others to accomplish the work we leaders ask them to perform.

Relationships are about "relating," or essentially passing both information and inspiration between people, so the quality of our work depends on these being strategic and meaningful. Creating an atmosphere of fear, distrust, or "me first" leads to scenarios where people withdraw from one another, with-holding information, wanting to be inspired but not to inspire. Less work gets done, and when it's done, things often slip through the cracks leading to poor quality, disappointed stakeholders and customers, and more.

To prevent this, strong relationships must be built first and foremost on trust, then respect, understanding, effective communication, support, compassion, and purposeful listening. In this sort of setting, people are inspired to give more of themselves, to contribute, and to achieve team and organi-zational goals. It is important to understand the value you and others bring to a team or project.

Actively listen to your employees and stakeholders so that you understand their potential, talents, and needs. Develop strategies and approaches to improve each relationship and then create a plan to grow and foster these relationships with trust, care, and compassion. You can offer your support by offering something of yourself, giving something genuine, whether it's guidance or collaboration on a project, compliments on work being well done, congratulations on successes achieved, or even trust in someone who wants to tackle a challenge in an innovative way. Taking care of the people you work with raises your value in their eyes and their dedication to you.

As a leader, you're in the position to reach out to others and establish meaningful relationships.

As you do this, you begin forming relationships between yourself and team members. But just as important, you begin setting the tone for other relationships to form. You can help to establish mentors and other partnerships within the overall organization. And as Jon Katzenbach, author of *The Wisdom of Teams* points out, "Find the Master Motivators." He says that these are the people within a group who have a natural talent for gaining emotional commitment from others. They can help inspire others, but can also give you insights into what motivates the group. You can use this to continue growing bonds with others that have real meaning for them.

Key Points:

- Cultivating relationships is critical to our ability to influence others to accomplish the work we leaders ask them to perform.
- Meaningful relationships are built first on trust, then respect, understanding, effective communication, support, compas-sion, and purposeful listening.
- Actively listen to your employees and stakeholders so that you understand their potential, talents, and needs.
- Develop strategies and approaches to improve each relationship and then create a plan to grow and foster these relationships.
- As a leader, you're in the position to reach out to others, one person at a time, and establish these relationships by collaborating and offering something genuine of yourself.

Written Exercises:

1. Identify Your Top 20 Core Network. These are the people who can help you get things done and get you to where you want to go. And you in turn offer the same help to them.

_____

_____

_____

_____

_____

_____

_____

_____

_____

_____

_____

_____

_____

_____

_____

_____

_____

2. Understand Each Person: What value does the person bring? What are her or his talents and strengths? What are her or his professional goals? How can you help? Who influences this person? What are this person's hot buttons? How would you describe this person's leadership and communication style?

_____

_____

_____

_____

_____

_____

_____

3. Develop an Ongoing Plan with strategies and initiatives to grow and foster these relationships.

_____

_____

_____

_____

_____

_____

_____

Chapter Reflections and Notes

_____

_____

_____

_____

_____

_____

_____

_____

_____

_____

_____

_____

_____

_____

_____

_____

_____

_____

_____

Strategy #8:
Use Authentic Communication

When I talk with leaders about the importance of building professional relationships, I include the topics of trust, respect, support, and honestly caring about team members and colleagues. These must underlie everything you do in building relationships. But the cornerstone to all of these, and good leadership itself, is the ability to authentically communicate.

Most of you are already effective communicators. Executives work hard on their communication, taking various trainings and seminars such as public speaking, business writing, improvisation, and storytelling. But what does it look like to be a *great* communicator?

Authentic leaders speak the truth with courage and compassion in a way that strengthens relationships and builds them up, even when giving tough feedback or under pressure. Plus, their actions align with their word's integrity, which further builds trust. Use communication to accomplish the following:

- Make sure your team understands both the big picture and steps toward that larger goal.
- Show why they should care about these goals.
- Detail what is and isn't working.
- Brainstorm solutions to problems.
- Inspire the team toward the next milestones.
- Recognize accomplishments along the way.

Simple, inspirational, clear messages tailored to the audience and individual are delivered both formally and informally. All of this is very important. However, there are other critical components to communication. Let's explore these a bit.

Awareness of How Your Message is Being Received

You deliver a message according to your understanding, judgment, perceptions, etc. When you deliver this message, you must be aware of how the other person is interpreting your message because they too have their understanding, judgments, and perceptions. Every person sees the world through a different lens, with different emotions and experiences that shape their world view. But so often, we get stuck on trying to get our message out for various reasons, needing to prove we are right, perhaps lacking time, or moving from one activity to another. Whatever the reason, we cut off the dialogue. The result: recipients may hear our message in a different way than we intended.

Let's look at an example. Your VP announces an urgent conference call to all Directors for that afternoon because of some changes that will be taking place in the organization. The VP is behind on an important deadline for the President and will explain the details of the changes and answer questions on the conference call later that day.

Meanwhile, the Director (recipient) of the message feels anxious and thinks, "surely this must be bad news — downsizing or maybe a merger." The economy isn't good and your spouse was just laid off. Thinking back, your father lost his job the same way. This is your lens, and it colors the way you hear the message.

As a leader, you are responsible for the language and words you use and the messages that you deliver. As the recipient you are responsible for how you interpret the message. Each person receives and hears messages through many filters. Leaders need to deliver messages with clarity and precision, and know when to stand back, observe, and — as the next section shows — ask clarifying questions for deeper understanding, rather than making assumptions.

The Art of Questioning for Communication

According to Marilee Adams, executive coach and author of *Change Your Questions, Change Your Life: 10 Powerful Tools for Life and Work,* "Question Thinking (QT) helps us think productively rather than reactively, and to choose wisely rather than simply react. Building such a reliable capacity for thinking is central to the skills required for intentional and sustainable change, whether that change is sought in our professional or personal lives. Without these skills, our goals for change may be only wistful slogans that will never come to fruition."

At the center of QT is our ability to direct our own thinking by observing and assessing the questions we ask ourselves while trying to change something or problem solve — whether it be putting out a fire at work, restructuring an organization, leading your team to better results, or managing personal problems. Adams categorizes thinking as Learner mode or Judger mode, then teaches how to design new questions for better relation-ships and results. This is about leaving your ego out of the conversation. There isn't any judgment, right or wrong, but through the art of the conversation, asking better questions, and listening to understand each other, better ideas and solutions arise.

Listening, Emotions, and Body Language

We all know the old adage, "You have two ears and one mouth. Use them in that proportion." Listening is a central part of communication that's too often forgotten and undervalued. Active listening with purpose and great emotional intelligence opens up dialogue. Listen for what is not being said too. Listening not only makes others feel like they're contributing; it makes them feel as if they're supported and understood in their work, especially when you respond to their spoken needs.

Great leaders also choose their words carefully, and they remember not to communicate from a place of anger, which goes back to the management of emotions that we talked about as part of Emotional Intelligence. Ineffective leaders unfortunately feel the need to lambaste team members for errors, causing embarrassment and resentment, rather than hearing the problems at hand and working with them to find solutions. In his famous book *How to Win Friends and Influence People*, Dale Carnegie tells us the story of Lincoln writing a letter, while angry, to one of the generals that had let him down ... and then never sending the letter. He knew not to communicate from a place of anger, but from a place of constructive efforts.

More than this, pay careful attention to your body language and tone of voice. Non-verbal communication accounts for about 93% of your message. In *Radical Collaboration* by James W. Tamm and Ronald J. Luyet, the authors state, "When any nonverbal behavior contradicts what is said in a message, the nonverbal behavior is more likely to determine how the message is understood. People trying to communicate a message that they have doubts about had better pay particular attention to their body language and tone of voice."

As you can see, communication is about much more than the words we say, and if we want to become great leaders, we need to work on all the skills that communication involves.

Key Points:

- Authentic Leaders speak the truth with courage and compassionately in a way that strengthens relationships, even when giving tough feedback.
- Choose your words carefully and align words with your actions. This builds trust.
- Be aware that people interpret messages through many filters. Observe and ask great questions to understand, brainstorm, and solve relationship and business issues rather than staying stuck in a power struggle or proving "you are right."
- Listen actively and purposely to understand. Be conscious of body language and tone of voice especially when under pressure. Nonverbal communication accounts for 93% of your message.
- Speak simply, clearly, and powerfully.
- This process will develop and build your trust and integrity muscle.

Written Exercises:

1. How can you be more aware of your language and communication, especially under pressure?

_____

_____

_____

_____

_____

2. How important is it for you to be right or look good vs. listening, understanding, and asking questions to come up with the best ideas/solutions?

_____

_____

_____

_____

_____

_____

3. What conflicts are you avoiding at work or in professional relationships because you have not been open and honest? How can you strengthen this relationship by being authentic?

_____

_____

_____

_____

_____

_____

4. What are key messages and information that your organization communicates well? Poorly? How can you address the weak areas? What can you do to improve communication up, down, and across your organization?

_____

_____

_____

5. Think of a time when you received a message that you interpreted through your filter/lens? What was happening in your career at that time?

_____

_____

_____

_____

_____

_____

_____

_____

_____

_____

_____

Chapter Reflections and Notes

_____

_____

_____

_____

_____

_____

_____

_____

_____

_____

_____

_____

_____

_____

_____

_____

_____

_____

_____

_____

_____

_____

Strategy #9:
Give Back

Giving back isn't just good PR for a business. It's also an advantage in every way for leaders, from its impact on you directly to your teams to making positive changes on the greater world around you.

Giving back is more than simply putting part of our financial success toward others, but actually giving of our time and the skills we accumulate with our success. This may mean becoming a mentor to others, not only within your own teams — which of course continues to accelerate business growth — but also to community business leaders and perhaps to youth groups, inspiring future leaders to have the right attitudes and understandings of what it means to succeed. Building the strength of your community generally supports your own business indirectly, and as any good teacher knows, you'll learn as much from mentoring others as they learn from you. So the cycle of good continues.

Whether it's your time, skills, or money, giving back and serving others never just impacts those you give directly to. When we teach new skills, provide insights, increase another's resources, or in any other way improve the world's ability to provide useful goods and services, that kind of impact continues spreading and eventually — usually in unnoticed ways — reaches back to help you to in your own ongoing growth.

When I was responsible for Leadership Development, one of the leadership programs was a two day training on Building and Leading High Performing Teams. The first day of the program was held in a classroom setting. The managers learned theories and developed a deeper understanding of how to build and lead high performing teams. Then the same day, the managers applied the theory learned in class and together built a team building day for children. What better way to apply these new skills than to take this new skill set out into the community and create a positive experience for children?

On day two, we partnered with a caring organization that helps young people, especially those in need, reach their full potential. These managers volunteered their time and talent, applied the principles they learned in class, and led a dynamic, fun-filled team day for these children. This was a great learning experience for everyone. It gave high potential managers the opportunity to participate in a training that would maximize their leadership capability and performance while giving back to society and improving the quality of lives. And the children learned the value of team work in a positive, caring environment while having fun.

As a leader, I was thrilled to be able to bring such a high value program to further develop the organization's future leaders and give back to society at the same time. Also, I felt deep gratitude, realizing that without the support of the VP of Talent Management and the Executive Team, this innovative leader-ship program wouldn't have taken place. It was life enhancing for everyone involved!

Importantly, there's another very direct benefit to you as a leader when you give back. As you discover what's important to you and what inspires you — your most important values — you can begin giving back in ways that support those values. Maybe you pass them along through your teaching, or you give to charities that best promote them. In any case, your business success becomes something much more than financial. It waters the roots of those values in the world and helps to grow this into a world of your own making to the degree that you contribute.

By giving back, you help shape future leaders and the entire world around you.

When the things that are most important to us grow as the result of what we do beyond our organization, we wake up feeling happier about the day before us, and there is no better energy to work with or to share with others as we walk this path of leadership. Einstein said, "The world we have created is a product of our way of thinking." Importantly, the more you put into ventures that support your values, the more those ventures will have the resources to attract still other people, and success will grow upon success and plant these values ever deeper into your community.

There is no better energy to work with or to share with others as we walk the path of leadership, sharing our hearts, giving a hand, helping others step into their higher purpose and making a positive difference in the world.

Key Points:

- Giving back is more than simply putting part of our financial success toward others, but actually giving of our time and the skills to make a greater contribution, making a lasting positive difference.
- What we contribute to the world around us continues spreading and eventually — usually in unnoticed ways — reaches back to help you and others in ongoing growth.
- As you support things that grow your own values in the world, you'll find yourself more personally inspired by your work, which is allowing you to accomplish this.

Written Exercises:

1. How do you want to be remembered in the world? What did you stand for as a leader? How did you serve others?

_____

_____

_____

_____

_____

2. What cause/charity inspires you, interests you the most? It could be a cause inside or outside of your organization. Who can help you get involved?

_____

_____

_____

_____

_____

3. How can you inspire and support employees and colleagues to contribute in ways that matter to them as a way to develop future leaders?

_____

_____

_____

_____

_____

Chapter Reflections and Notes

_____

_____

_____

_____

_____

_____

_____

_____

_____

_____

_____

_____

_____

_____

_____

_____

_____

_____

_____

_____

_____

_____

Strategy #10:
Bring Happiness to Work

I discussed Emotional Intelligence in an earlier portion of this book. You can't change anything until you are first aware, mindful of your emotions. In the *Art of Happiness*, the Dalai Lama and Howard Cutler mention that "the first step in seeking happiness is learning." They go on to say how important it is to be aware of how negative emotions harm us and positive emotions help us.

Of course we can't be happy all the time, but negative emotions are not good for you or the people around you. Even if you think you are not showing your negative feelings, your mood will not be the same as when you are happy, and this brings others' moods down and creates stress. So it's important to put in the effort to switch thoughts from negative to positive. The Dalai Lama finds that mental states such as kindness and compassion lead to better communication, psychological health, and happiness.

Martin Seligman is a pioneer in Positive Psychology and in *Learned Optimism* he mentions three ways to be happier: aim to have as much positive emotion as possible and learn the skills to magnify these emotions; identify your strengths and talents and use them as much as you can in your work; and then, to live a more meaningful life, use these strengths and talents to serve something bigger than yourself.

Depending on who you speak to, the subject of happiness at work will reap you many different reactions. Recent research, however, shows how importantly it figures in to an organization's bottom line. For instance, a 2008 study by Gallup Healthways showed that employees who are less satisfied with their lives stay home from work an average 1.25 more days per month, which equals 15 days of decreased productivity per year. More Gallup research shows that retail stores whose employees score high on life satisfaction sell $21 more in earnings per square foot of space.

According to Shawn Achor, founder of the corporate strategy firm Good Think and the author of *The Happiness Advantage*, other research shows that a positive mindset raises performance with nearly all workplace talents including productivity, engagement, and creativity.

I once worked with a Vice President who made sure employees who attended corporate trainings could unwind in the evening after long days of training when they were away from home. He had a Wii installed so people could gather and laugh after long days of training. This same VP also scheduled after work socials at a nearby restaurant so employees in his department could get to know each other better outside of work. From personal experience, it was fun to take my direct reports out to lunch or dinner to get to know them better. Gestures like these demonstrate kindness and can really decrease stress and boost morale. There are plenty of ways to have fun at work: learn to take yourself less seriously, laugh at yourself more, choose a positive attitude, and spread happiness by doing small acts of kindness.

Key Points:

- The Dalai Lama feels that happiness can be learned. He also finds that mental states such as kindness and compassion lead to better communication, psychological health, and happiness.
- In *Learned Optimism*, Martin Seligman mentions three ways to be happier: aim to have as much positive emotion as possible and learn the skills to magnify these emotions; identify your strengths and talents and use them as much as you can in your work; and then, to live a more meaningful life, use these strengths and talents to serve something bigger than yourself.
- A 2008 study by Gallup Healthways showed that employees who are less satisfied with their lives stay home from work an average 1.25 more days per month, which equals 15 days of decreased productivity per year.
- Research shows that a positive mindset raises performance with nearly all workplace talents including productivity, engagement, and creativity.

Written Exercises:

1. What can you do when you need a boost of happiness and optimism? Here are some examples:

   - Go out with colleagues for lunch or dinner.
   - Take a brisk walk outside at lunch to recharge.
   - Place pictures of happy memories on your desk.
   - Give a smile or compliment.
   - Keep a gratitude journal.
   - Play your favorite music.
   - Bring in a favorite snack for everyone.
   - Take a 5 minute relaxation break and stretch at your desk.

   _____

   _____

   _____

   _____

2. What ways can you use your strengths and talents every day to boost happiness and positive emotions at work.

   _____

   _____

   _____

   _____

3. For Authentic Coaching Newsletters, questionnaires, and resources, visit Dr. Seligman's Authentic Happiness at:

http://www.authentichappiness.sas.upenn.edu/Default.aspx

Chapter Reflections and Notes

_____

_____

_____

_____

_____

_____

_____

_____

_____

_____

_____

_____

_____

_____

_____

_____

_____

_____

_____

Conclusion

Any leadership role can be an exciting adventure, not only in business success but in personal growth and in contributions to the people and the community around you. I urge you to live in awareness, because living on autopilot keeps you from reaching your full potential. The most important asset you have is self- awareness, knowing your values and who you are on the inside. With this internal compass, your higher purpose unfolds, and you will make a greater impact in everything you do.

Also, coaching, supporting, understanding, and guiding your employees in the moment is how you become a more powerful leader and catalyst for change. People will feel your enthusiasm and genuineness when you are completely present with them. Your belief in their talent will instill a deeper confidence and commitment to be their absolute best.

Every intentional step you take in becoming a more conscious *leader* makes the j o u r n e y that much more purpose driven and fulfilling. So it's important that we never stop in our commitment to learning about leadership and applying what we learn to what we do. Leadership is a lifelong journey to becoming a beacon of light and love to those you serve, forging a path of hope that brings a brighter future, especially in challenging times.

By exploring together some of the key elements of leadership — from personal values that direct your choices ... to building better teams by combining individual strengths, supporting people with Emotional Intelligence, leading with your head and heart, staying true to authentic communication, and more ... and all the way on to completing the circle by giving back — I hope this book has offered you one or more valuable points to ponder. I hope you've also been able to make use of some of the Written Exercises, as these take the words out of your mind and into the real world to practice. When you bring this kind of laser sharp focus and commitment to 1 or 2 areas where you can make the greatest impact, it will be transformative, moving things in the right direction. And isn't greater success and happiness worth 30 minutes of your time each day? If you think so, then consider committing to this work starting today.

Besides learning and application, we all need mentors and sponsors in our lives as well. I encourage you to make sure you're building that all-important trusted network of people who can support and be supported by you in different areas of your career and personal life. And if you ever feel that a 'thinking partner' or coach would help to focus your efforts, encourage the right actions, hold you accountable, and propel you to the next levels in your own career, I hope you'll feel free to reach out to me so I can lend a hand, empowering you on your leadership journey.

My best wishes to you on your path to becoming your absolute best.

Teresa Shaffer, CEC, CPC
Shaffer Executive Coaching, LLC
www.ShafferExecutiveCoaching.com

About The Author

Teresa is passionate about helping you to achieve your biggest aspirations – to boldly step into your authentic power and act with the confidence and courage that will help make you the best you can be.

Teresa's unique approach helps organizations to fulfill their purpose through the development of transformational leaders and aligned teams. She is committed to partnering with individuals to co-create more conscious, diverse and inclusive organizations by having a balanced embrace of masculine and feminine qualities in order to lift their organizations to a higher plane.

At the core of Teresa's work is a set of values, skills, and practical tools that enables leaders and organizations to achieve extraordinary results.

Partnering with Teresa, will help you maximize your talents, strengths, and leadership capabilities to achieve greater success and happiness.

If you have questions on her coaching philosophy, fees, or schedule, please contact Teresa at:

www.ShafferExecutiveCoaching.com
teresa@shafferexecutivecoaching.com

or

917.426.5308.

.

www.ingramcontent.com/pod-product-compliance
Lightning Source LLC
Chambersburg PA
CBHW071622170526
45166CB00003B/1162